Mechanic Mike's Machines

Trains

ЧС4-072

Franklin Watts
This edition published in the UK in 2016 by The Watts Publishing Group

Copyright © 2014 David West Children's Books

Designed and illustrated by David West

Dewey number 625.2
PB ISBN: 978 1 4451 5179 3

Printed in Malaysia

Franklin Watts
An imprint of
Hachette Children's Group
Part of The Watts Publishing Group
Carmelite House
50 Victoria Embankment
London EC4Y 0DZ

An Hachette UK Company.
www.hachette.co.uk

www.franklinwatts.co.uk

MECHANIC MIKE'S MACHINES TRAINS
was produced for Franklin Watts by
David West Children's Books, 6 Princeton Court, 55 Felsham Road, London SW15 1AZ

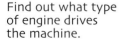

Mechanic Mike says:
Mike will tell you something more about the machine.

 Find out what type of engine drives the machine.

 Discover something you didn't know.

 Is it fast or slow? Top speeds are given here.

 How many crew or people does it carry?

 Get your amazing fact here!

Contents

Early American steam **locomotives** like the 'General', built in 1855, had a tall chimney stack and a cow catcher on the front. This was to clear the rail line of anything that might derail the train.

Early steam trains, such as the 'General', could reach 32.1 kilometres per hour in short bursts.

Steam trains usually had a crew of at least two people, the driver and the fireman, who kept the fire in the boiler fed with coal.

Did you know the 'General' is famous for the 'Great Locomotive Chase' during the American Civil War? Union soldiers stole the train and were chased by other trains full of Confederate soldiers.

It has a steam engine.

Chimney stack

Boiler

Rods

Piston

Cow catcher

4

Steam

The earliest locomotives were powered by steam. Coal or wood was burned to heat up water in a boiler to make steam.

Mechanic Mike says:
Steam from the boiler pushed pistons inside cylinders. Rods attached to the pistons turned the wheels.

W. & A.R.R.

The biggest **diesels** were the American Union Pacific Centennial locomotives. They were 30 metres long.

 Diesel trains can be fast. The InterCity 125 diesel train, used for passenger service in the UK, is the fastest diesel train at 231 kilometres per hour.

 A former Santa Fe F45, in Montana, USA, has been converted into a holiday lodge where four people can stay.

 This diesel-electric EMD F45 has a crew of two.

 This EMD F45 has a 20-cylinder diesel engine powering electric motors.

Mechanic Mike says:
Diesel trains that power electric motors are sometimes called diesel-electric trains.

Diesel

Diesel locomotives are powered by diesel engines. In some trains the engine powers electric motors that turn the wheels.

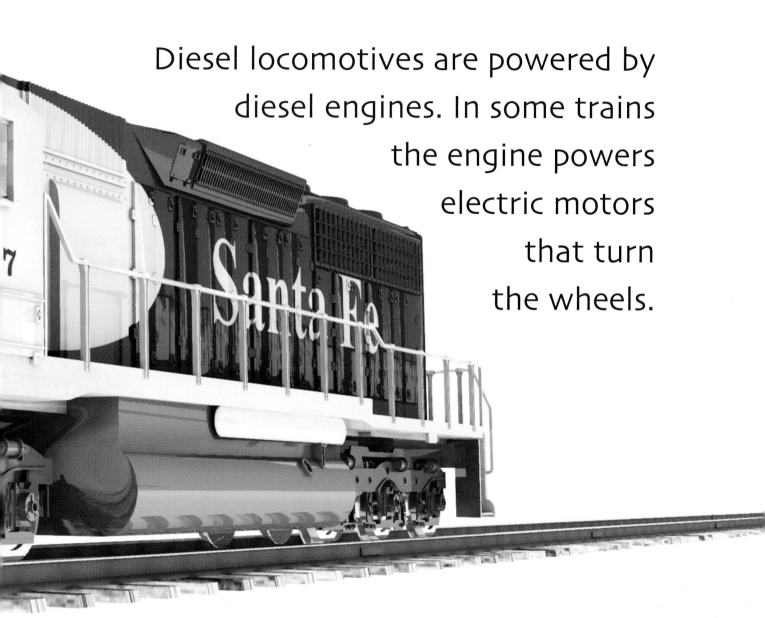

Electric

Electric locomotives are powered by electricity from a third rail or from overhead lines. Flexible rods called **pantographs** on the roof of the locomotive contact the overhead wire to transfer the electricity.

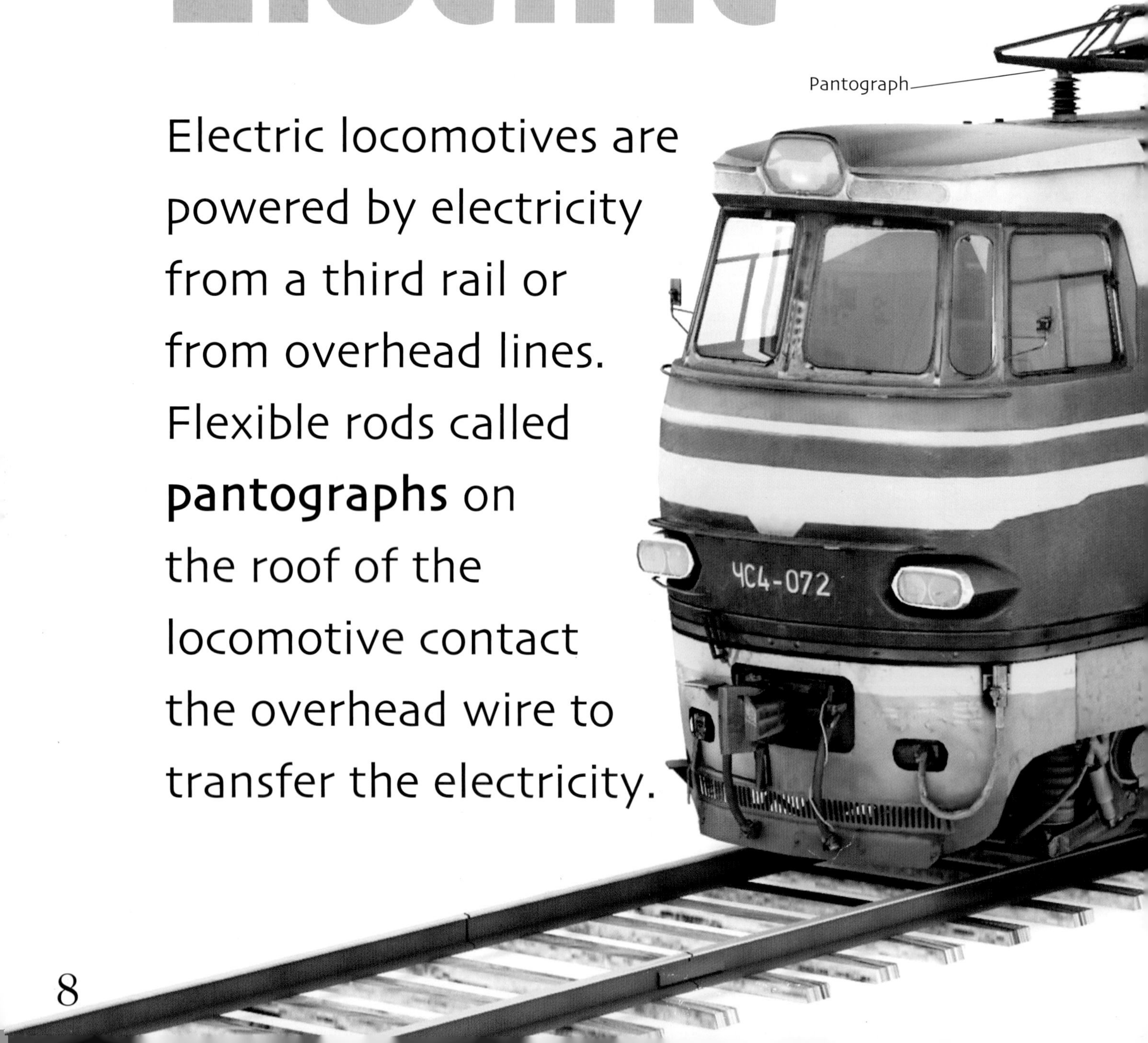

Pantograph

ЧС4-072

Mechanic Mike says:
At the flick of a switch this locomotive can travel forwards or backwards.

This ChS4-012 pulled passenger carriages between Moscow and Odessa, in Russia.

Although electric locomotives can be fast, this Russian Skoda ChS4's top speed is only 160 kilometres per hour.

The newest model of this locomotive can pull 32 passenger carriages.

Did you know that the ChS4-012 has been retired and is in the Kiev museum of railway transport?

It is powered by electric motors.

9

High-Speed

High-speed trains carry passengers on special tracks over long distances. They travel at about 320 kilometres per hour.

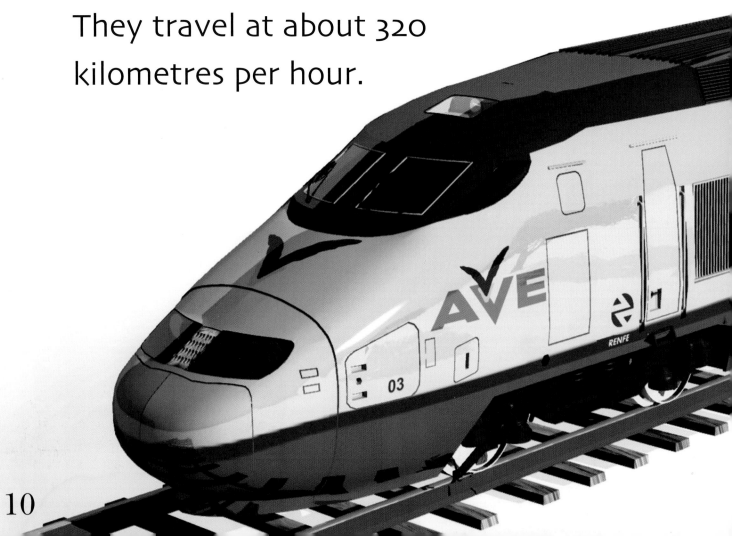

The Chinese CRH380A is the fastest high-speed train in service. It can travel at 350 kilometres per hour.

It is powered by electric motors.

High-speed trains have only one driver.

Did you know that the French TGV set a train speed record of 574.8 kilometres per hour?

This Spanish high-speed train travels at up to 310 kilometres per hour on journeys between Madrid and Seville in Spain.

Mechanic Mike says:
China has the world's longest high-speed rail line. It runs 2,208 kilometres from Beijing in the north to Shenzhen on the southern coast.

Freight

Trains don't just carry people. They are an inexpensive way of transporting all sorts of goods from oil, gas and coal to grain, cattle and **ore**.

Diesel locomotive

Mechanic Mike says:
In some countries 'rolling highway' trains are used. These freight trains have special wagons that allow trucks to drive on to the train and drive off again when they arrive at their destination.

Freight wagon

Did you know the Daqin Railway in China transports more than 1 million metric tons of coal to the east coast every day?

Freight trains are usually limited to about 120.7 kilometres per hour.

Loads can be 130 metric tons per wagon and thousands of tons per train.

Freight trains are normally pulled by diesel locomotives.

Some freight trains can be over 7 kilometres long.

13

The first **rapid transit system** was the London Underground, which opened in 1863.

 Did you know that the busiest rapid transport systems are the Tokyo Subway, the Seoul Metropolitan Subway, and the Moscow Metro? The New York City Subway has the record for the most stations.

 The train's top speed is 80 kilometres per hour. Its average speed is 40 kilometres per hour.

 The Danish Copenhagen Metro system carries more than 137,000 people per day. Each three-carriage train holds up to 96 seated and 204 standing passengers.

 The train is powered by electric motors. The electricity is picked up from a third, electrified, rail.

Rapid Transit

Rapid transit trains carry passengers around **urban** areas. The trains run frequently and are designed to carry lots of people. They often travel on lines above roads and underground.

Mechanic Mike says:
Some rapid transit trains, like this Copenhagen Metro in Denmark, are completely automated and have no driver.

The Colorado Rail Bilevel rail cars are 6 metres tall.

Did you know that some countries, such as the UK, don't have bilevel trains because they won't fit under some of the bridges?

Some high-speed bilevel trains travel faster than 160 kilometres per hour.

A four-car set can carry around 400 people.

This multiple unit train has self-propelled carriages. Electricity drives the electric motors that are in many of the carriages.

Bilevel

Mechanic Mike says:
Bilevel trains are used in many countries around the world. This one runs in the Netherlands.

These tall trains, also known as double-deckers, have two levels for passengers. This allows them to carry more people in a shorter train. A longer train would need longer platforms to be built.

Tram

These rail vehicles run on tracks along city streets, and sometimes on special rail lines, too. Most trams today use electric power, usually supplied by a pantograph.

The first tram was horse-drawn. It first ran in 1807 between Swansea and the Mumbles in South Wales.

Did you know that some trams, called cable cars, are pulled by cables?

Modern trams may be up to 72 metres long and carry 510 passengers.

Most modern trams are powered by electric motors.

Trams' speed limits vary, depending on the country. It is usually around 80 kilometres per hour.

Mechanic Mike says: Trams are also known as trolley buses or streetcars.

Some monorail designs have the trains hanging from a single rail rather than sitting on top of it.

Monorails are usually quite slow. The Tokyo Monorail runs at 80 kilometres per hour.

The first monorail to carry passengers operated during the 1820s in Hertfordshire.

Unknown Node

The busiest monorail line is the Tokyo Monorail. It carries more than 300,000 passengers daily.

Almost all modern monorails are powered by electric motors.

Mechanic Mike says:
Monorails, like this one in Las Vegas, are popular with tourists as the height gives them a more **elevated** view of the city.

Monorail

Monorail

These trains run along one rail which is usually high above the ground. The train has rubber wheels that can grip the monorail, allowing it to go up and down slopes.

Maglev

Maglev trains use powerful **electromagnets** to hover above the rail. The magnets are also used to move the train. As there is no contact with the rail, these trains are very smooth, quiet and fast.

SNT

The first commercial maglev train was called 'MAGLEV' and started in 1984 near Birmingham.

The highest recorded speed of a maglev train is 581 kilometres per hour.

The top operational speed of this Shanghai Maglev train is 431 kilometres per hour. It is the world's fastest train in regular use.

The Shanghai Maglev can carry 244 people.

It uses electromagnetic propulsion.

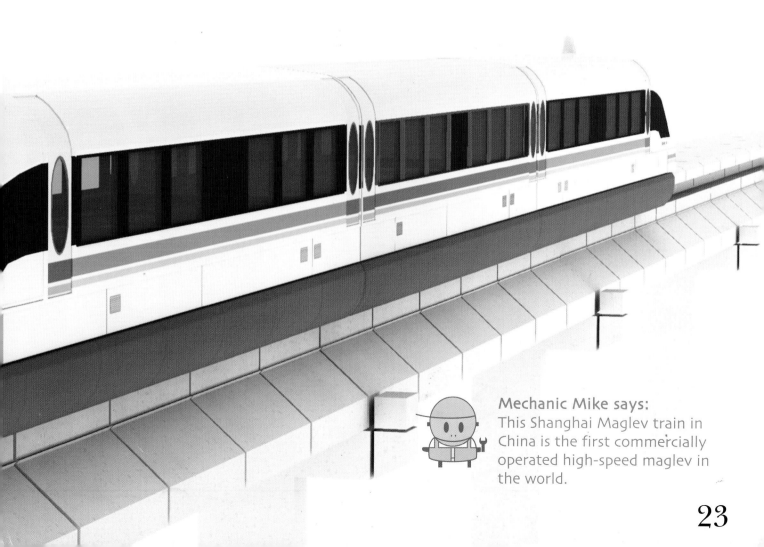

Mechanic Mike says:
This Shanghai Maglev train in China is the first commercially operated high-speed maglev in the world.

23

Glossary

diesel
A liquid fuel used in diesel engines. Diesel engines can be very powerful.

electromagnet
A magnet produced using electricity.

elevated
Higher than the surrounding area.

locomotive
The railway vehicle that pulls a train.

ore
Rocks that contain useful metal or minerals.

pantographs
Arms that connect a vehicle to overhead wires to transfer electric power.

rapid transit system
A rail passenger transport system in an urban area.

urban
A built-up area such as a city or town.

Index